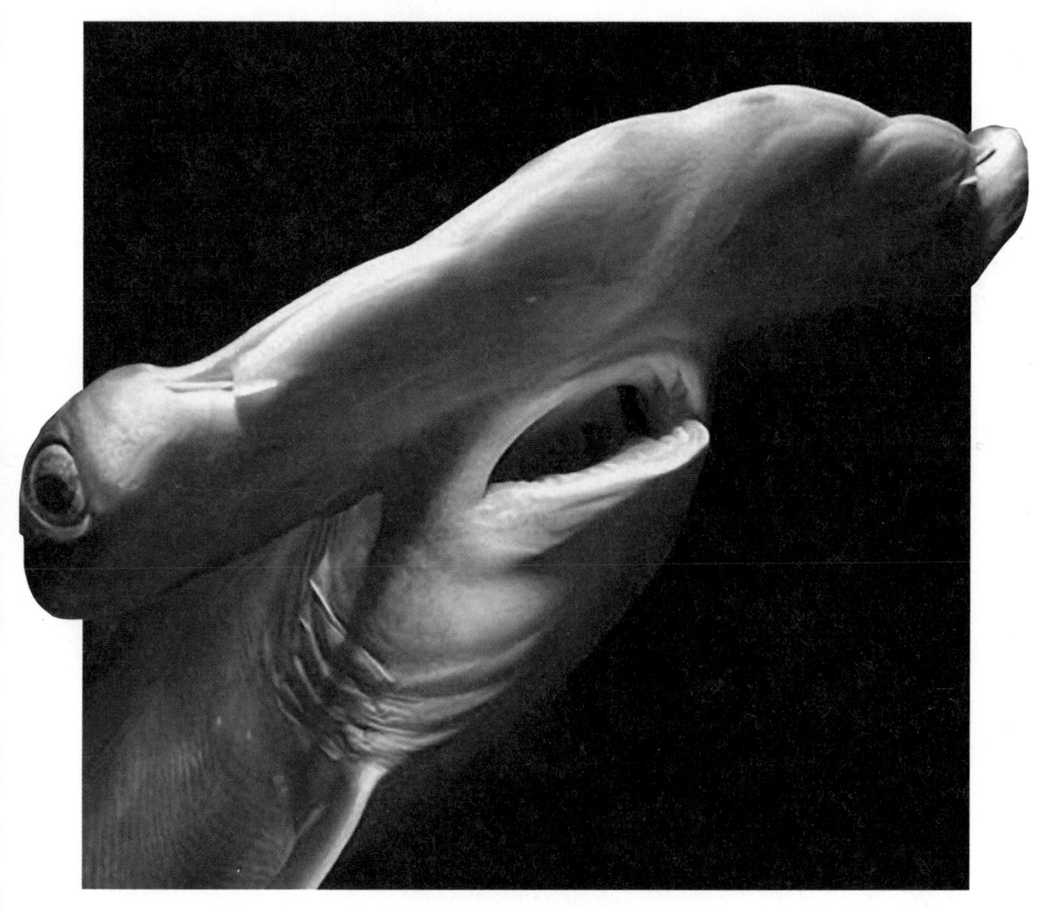

By Michael Candelaria

World Discovery Science Readers™

SCHOLASTIC INC.

New York • Toronto • London • Auckland • Sydney
Mexico City • New Delhi • Hong Kong • Buenos Aires

Great White Shark

Chapter 1

What Is a Shark?

Sharks have ruled Earth's oceans for about 450 million years. Sharks from long ago were fierce predators that could catch and eat just about any other animal. Early sharks were the most feared creatures in the ocean.

Modern sharks have most of the features that made their **ancestors** so powerful. Sharks today still rule the oceans.

Why have these meat-eating fish been so successful for so long? It is because their bodies are perfectly made for life in the sea.

One prehistoric shark is called the megalodon. Megalodons may have been more than 40 feet (12 m) long.

Great White Tooth

Megalodon Tooth

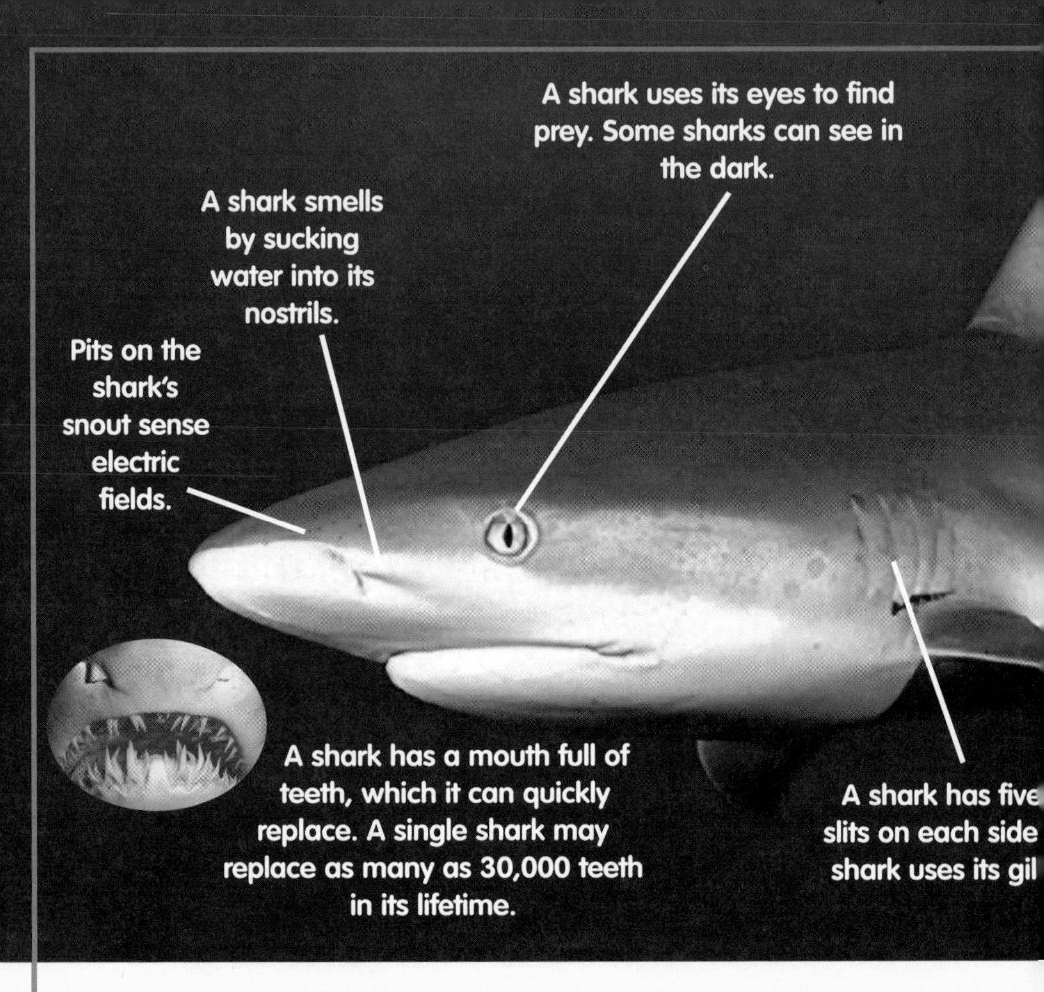

There are more than 460 species, or types, of sharks. Different species have different features. But most sharks have certain things in common. The picture on these pages shows the main parts of a shark's body.

Many sharks have jagged or **serrated** teeth.

Many sharks are dark on top and light underneath. This is called **countershading**.

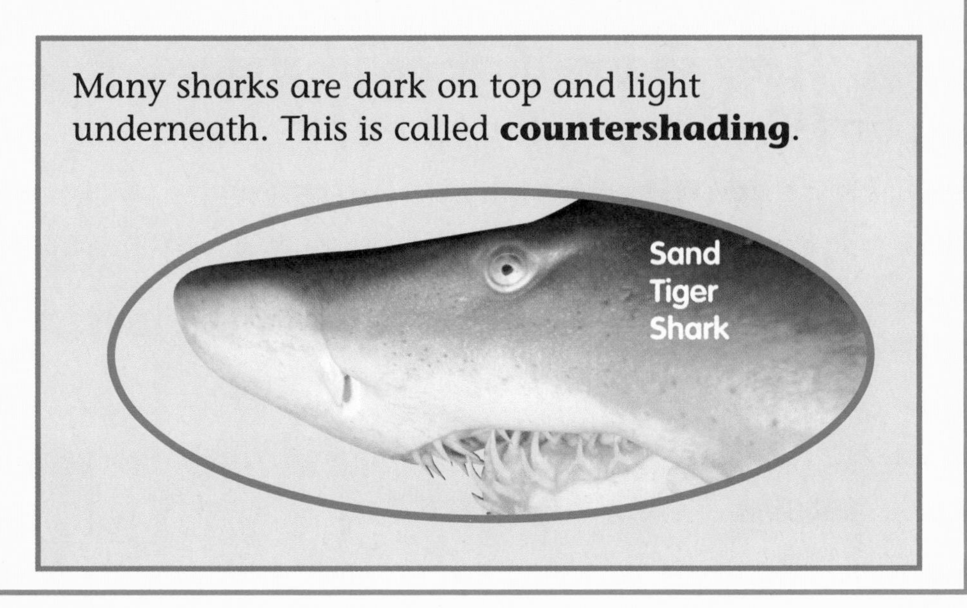

Sharks' bodies come in many different shapes. The most common shape looks like a torpedo. This shape is very **streamlined**, which means it glides easily through the water.

Wobbegong

Some sharks have flattened bodies. Wobbegong sharks lie on the sand. Their spotted skin matches the ocean floor and makes them very hard to see.

Some sharks have oddly shaped parts. Sawsharks, for example, have toothy **snouts** that look like saws. Hammerhead sharks have flat heads that poke out from both sides of their bodies.

Sawshark

Sharks come in many different sizes. Most sharks are between 3 and 10 feet (0.9 and 3 m) long. And the world's biggest shark is the whale shark.

Whale Shark

Whale sharks can grow as long as 48 feet (14.5 m), which is longer than a school bus! The spined pygmy shark is the world's smallest shark. It is just seven inches (18 cm) long. It would take more than 80 pygmy sharks to equal the length of one whale shark.

Sharks' skeletons are made of **cartilage**, not bone. People have cartilage in their ears and noses. Cartilage is strong, but it is softer than bone. It bends easily. This makes a shark's body very **flexible**.

Sharks can see, taste, touch, and hear, just like people do. But they also have extra senses that people do not have.

Smell is the shark's most powerful sense. A shark's sense of smell is hundreds of times stronger than a human's sense of smell. A shark might follow a blood trail for a mile (1.6 km) to reach a wounded animal.

Sharks also can feel **vibrations** in the water with the tiny hairs on their heads and the sides of their bodies. The hairs are connected to an organ called the **lateral line**. Vibrations make the hairs move. Then the lateral line organ sends messages to the shark's brain.

Many sharks have slit pupils. This type of eye pupil helps a shark see in dark water. Slit pupils also can close tightly to keep light out of a shark's sensitive eyes.

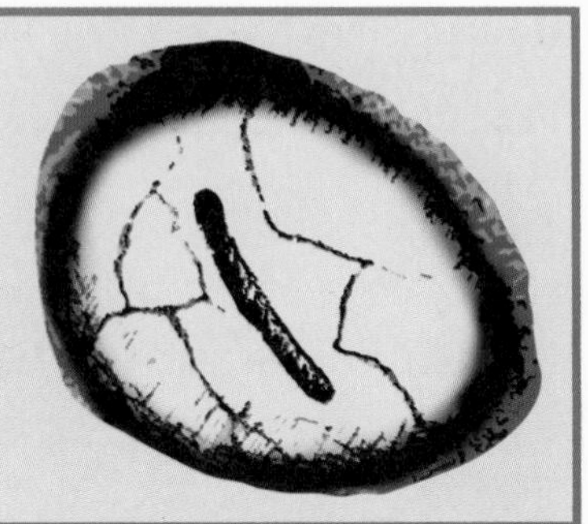

Great Hammerhead Shark

Sharks can also sense the tiny electrical charges given off by living animals. Hammerhead sharks use their electrical sense when they hunt. They swing their heads back and forth over a sandy area to find hidden prey.

Shark Egg

Chapter 2

The Life of a Shark

Sharks start their lives as babies, like all animals do. Baby sharks are called **pups**.

Shark pups of different species come into the world in different ways. Some, like silvertip sharks, are born live from female sharks. Others, like catsharks, hatch from eggs.

Shark pups look just like adults, but smaller. They are born with sharp little teeth, tiny perfect fins, and powerful bodies. They have everything they need to start their lives in the ocean.

Shark eggs are sometimes called "mermaid's purses." Curly strands at the eggs' corners cling to rocks and seaweed. This keeps the eggs from drifting away.

Life is hard for baby sharks. They must fight to survive from the moment they come into the world. Why? Pups are little at first, so they are often eaten by larger animals. Even their own mothers might eat them.

Shark pups of all species swim in shallow water to stay away from bigger creatures. But many pups get eaten anyway. Only half of all sharks reach one year of age. The chances of survival get better each year as a shark gets bigger and stronger. Being bigger helps a shark protect itself.

Most sharks can live 40 to 60 years, if they are very lucky. A few species can even live 150 years! But most sharks do not reach old age. Larger sharks or other creatures kill them long before they die of natural causes.

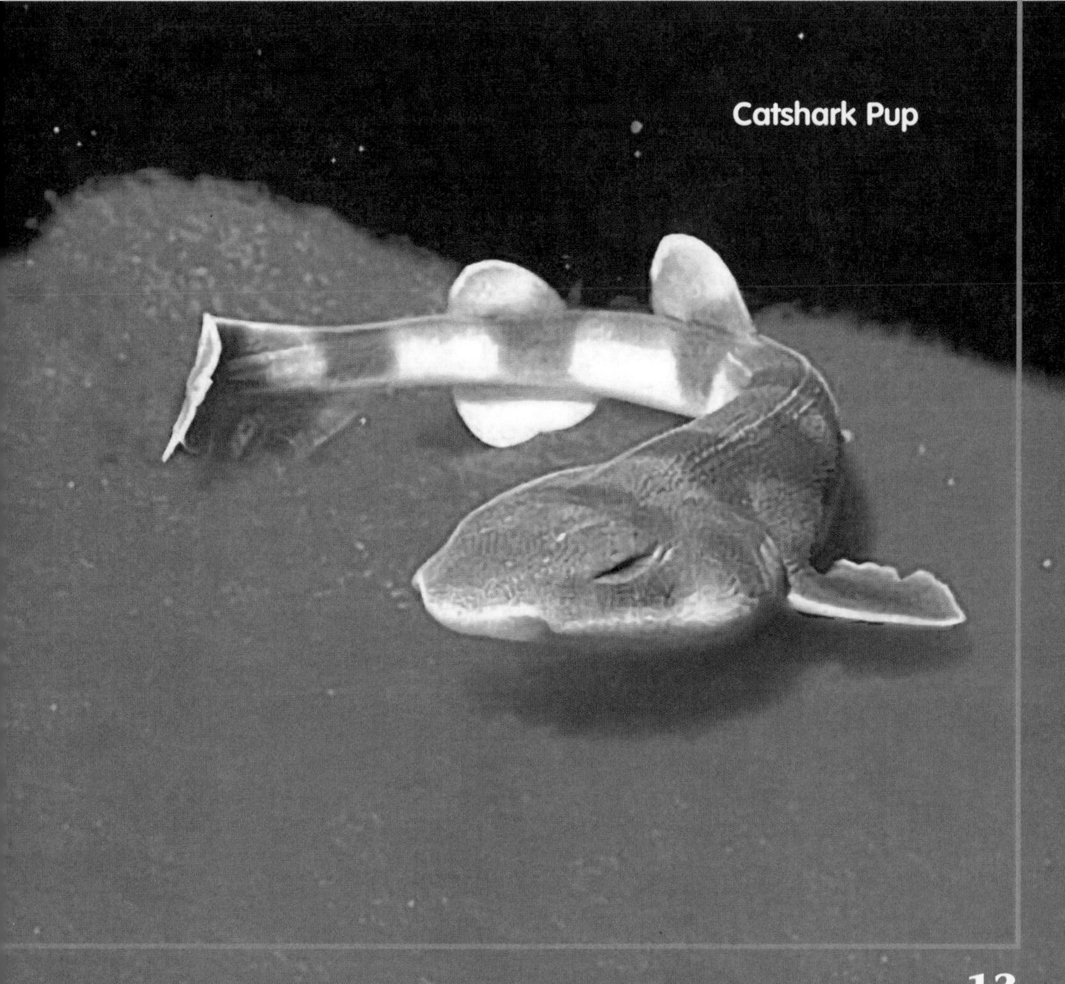

Catshark Pup

How can you tell a shark's age? Scientists look for certain clues to answer this question. Size is one thing they look for. Sharks continue to grow as long as they live, so really big sharks are always older sharks.

As sharks become older, they may also change their looks. A tiger shark pup, for example, has spotted markings that grow together to form stripes. But the stripes fade as the pup grows.

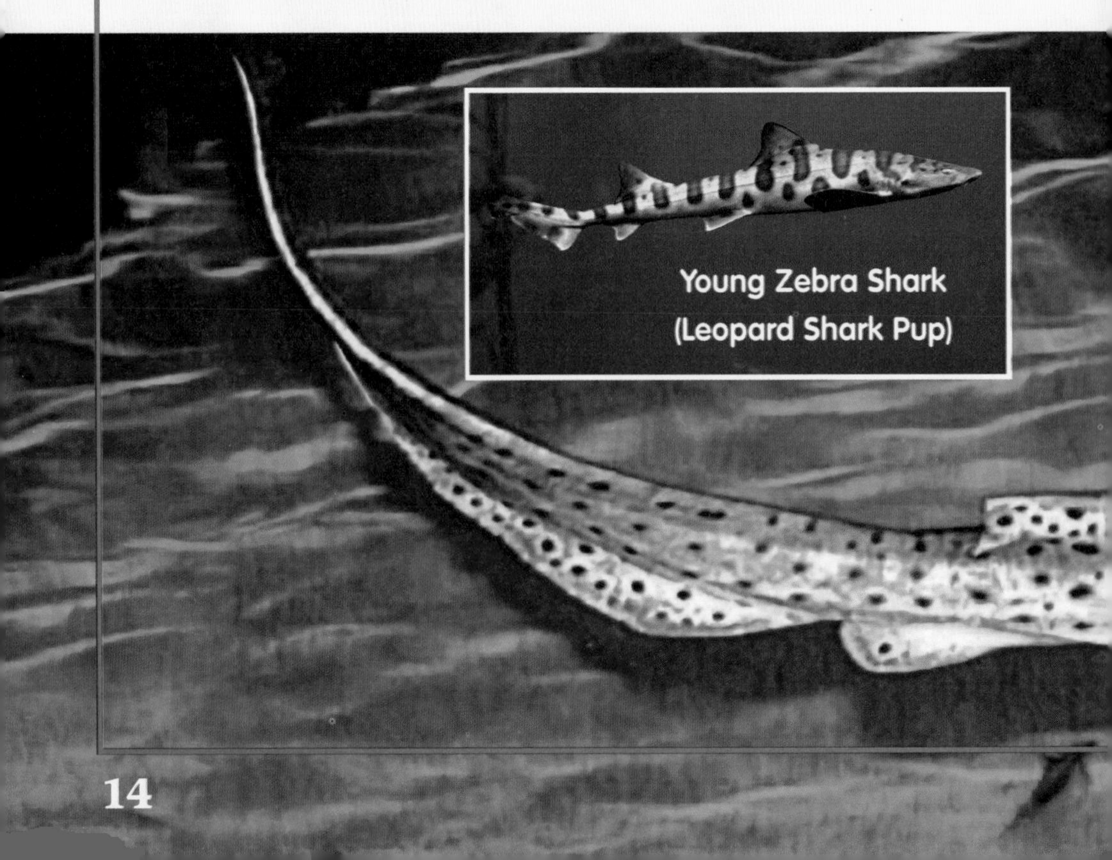

Young Zebra Shark (Leopard Shark Pup)

Zebra sharks also change the way they look. A young zebra shark has dark blotches on its skin. These blotches shrink into tiny spots as the shark grows. Adult zebra sharks are called leopard sharks because of their spots.

Sometimes scientists can tell a shark's age by counting growth rings in its backbone.

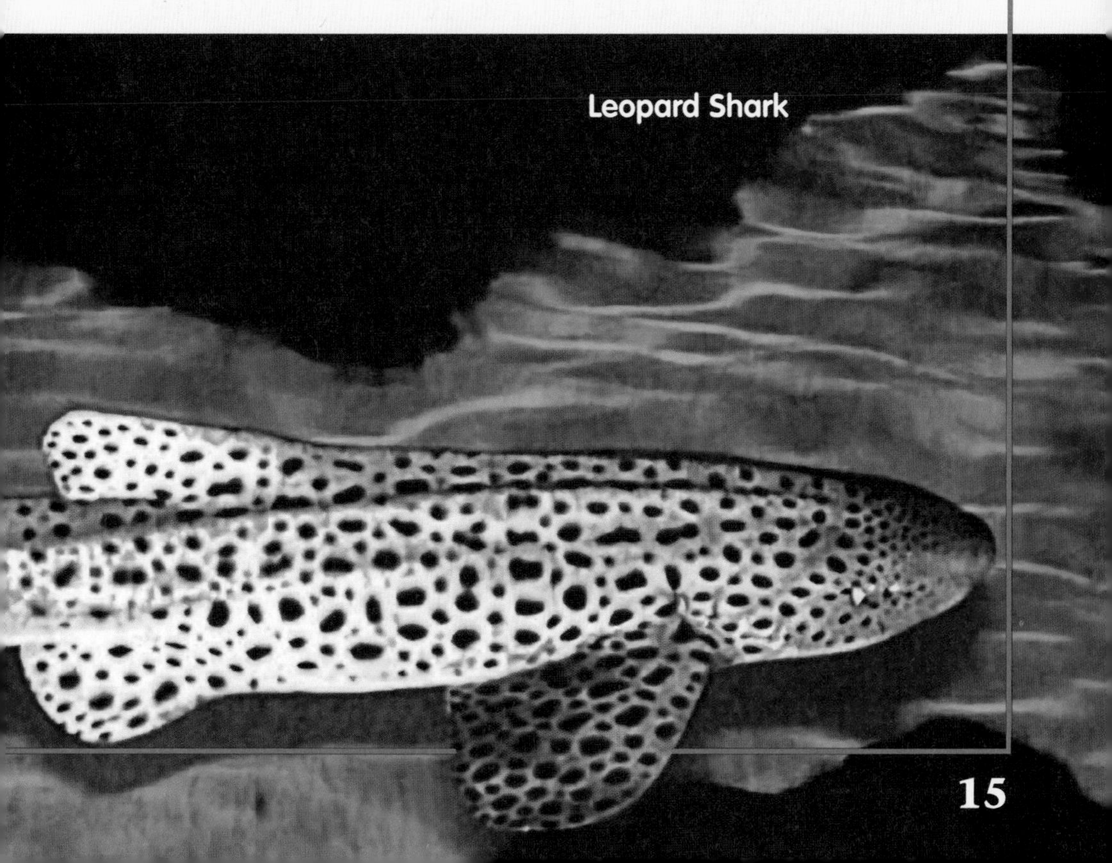

Leopard Shark

Chapter 3

Where Sharks Live

Sharks live in every single part of every ocean on Earth. No matter where you look in the world's oceans, you are sure to find a shark.

Some shark species travel, while others stay in one place for their whole lives. Some sharks like warm water and others like cold water. Some sharks are swimmers and others are bottom dwellers. Sharks just might pop up anywhere!

Most sharks live alone. But hammerheads are an exception. These sharks sometimes swim together in groups called schools. A hammerhead school may contain dozens of sharks.

Hammerhead Shark School

Sharks live everywhere from the freezing waters near the earth's poles to the warm seas of the equator. Water temperature influences where a shark will make its home.

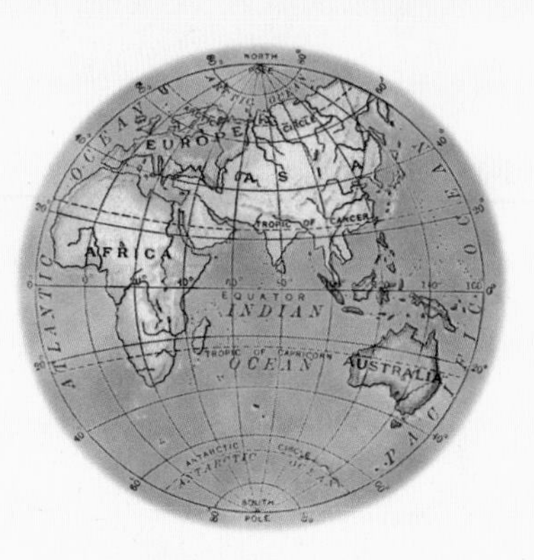

Bull sharks live in warm water. They are found in all **tropical** oceans. They also like rivers and lakes. Bull sharks have been seen in the Mississippi River and Lake Nicaragua in Central America, among other places. These sharks can be recognized by their short, wide noses.

Bull Shark

Thresher Shark

Thresher sharks like water that is neither too hot nor too cold. They are found in the Atlantic, Pacific, and Indian oceans. A thresher shark's tail is as long as the rest of its body. The shark uses its long tail like a whip to stun fish and other prey.

Goblin sharks like cold water. They are sluggish bottom dwellers and are rarely seen. Goblin sharks live at great depths of more than 3,000 feet (900 m). They can reach lengths of 11 feet (3.3 m).

A shark's dorsal fin sticks out of the water when the shark swims near the surface.

Different sharks live at different depths. Some stay near the water's surface and swim all the time. Others settle on the bottom of the ocean and spend a lot of time being still.

Sharks that live near the surface are seen more often than sharks that live on the sea floor. Basking sharks are surface swimmers. They are the second largest shark species and can grow up to 25 feet (7.6 m) long. Basking sharks sometimes bump into small boats. They also get tangled in fishing nets.

Basking Shark

Angel sharks live on the ocean floor, so they are not seen as often. Angel sharks have flat bodies and are slow swimmers that catch prey through surprise attacks. Many angel sharks are also caught as prey by other creatures, including tiger and hammerhead sharks.

Angel Shark

Sharks also vary in their movement. Some sharks are travelers that move from place to place. Other sharks stay close to home.

Blue sharks like to travel long distances. These graceful sharks can swim up to 40 miles (64 km) per hour. They **migrate** across oceans and are found all over the world.

Blue Shark

A blue shark was tagged and released by researchers near New York. Later it was found near Brazil. That blue shark swam 3,740 miles (6,000 km)!

Blacktip Shark

Blacktip sharks also travel, but not as far as blue sharks do. Blacktip sharks usually swim near coastlines. They are often found in shallow waters and near coral reefs.

Horn sharks do not swim much. They sit on the ocean floor and live in one area throughout their lives. One horn shark stayed in the same spot for more than 11 years!

Horn Shark

Chapter 4

Deadly Hunters

All sharks are **carnivores**. They eat the flesh of other animals. Sharks easily catch all the food they need to survive. Sometimes sharks are even called "killing machines" because they are such good hunters.

Sharks are not picky. They will eat just about any living creature. Fish, eels, seals, jellyfish, seabirds, lobsters, and even other sharks make good meals for a hungry shark.

Sometimes sharks eat things that are not food. License plates, paper cups, reindeer antlers, and other strange objects have been found in tiger sharks' stomachs.

Great White Shark

Different sharks have different ways of catching food. Sharks use hunting styles that match their bodies and the way they live.

Mako sharks, for example, live far from land. So they must catch swimming prey in open water. Makos can swim up to 60 miles (97 km) per hour. They are the world's fastest sharks. These speedy sharks easily catch fish, squid, smaller sharks, and other swimming sea creatures.

Leopard sharks have a different way of getting food. Leopard sharks live in shallow water, and they like to grab shellfish off the ocean floor. This is called **bottom feeding**.

Leopard Shark

A few types of sharks, including whale sharks, basking sharks, and megamouth sharks, eat plankton. **Plankton** is a mixture of tiny fish, squid, and other creatures. Sharks catch plankton by pushing seawater through large gills. The water escapes, but the plankton gets caught in special plates. The shark then swallows the trapped animals. This way of eating is called **filter feeding**.

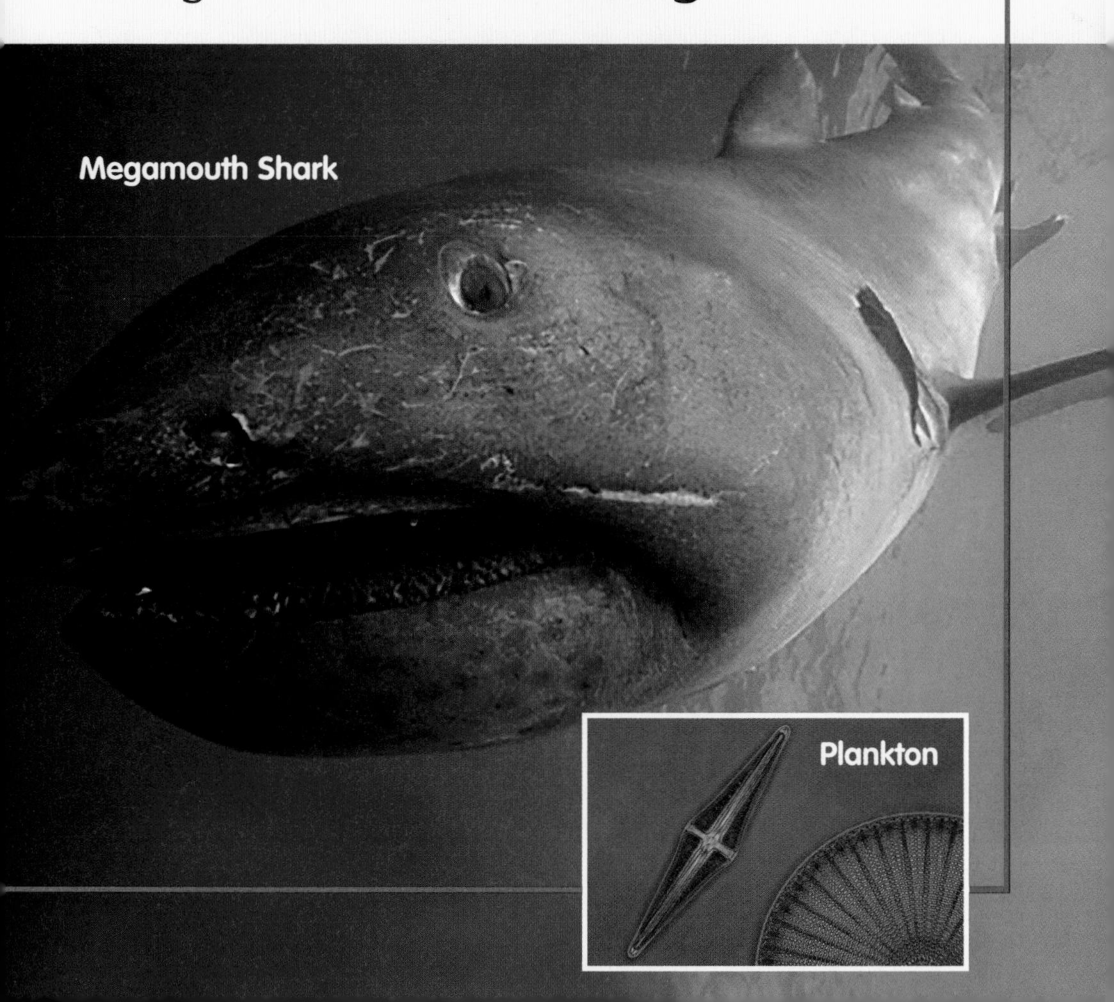

Some people are afraid they will be bitten by a shark. It is true that sharks can be dangerous to people. But sharks do not bite for the fun of it. They bite only when they get hungry. And humans are not part of the shark's diet, so they are not usually attacked.

A diver in a protective cage gets a closer look at a great white shark.

Sharks bite only about 100 people each year. More people die from lightning strikes and bee stings than shark attacks.

Great white sharks are responsible for most human attacks. These sharks have sharp teeth that easily cut human flesh. They are the only sharks that can lift their heads out of the water to look for food. Most great whites are about 16 feet (5 m) long, but they can grow as big as 23 feet (7 m). They can weigh up to 7,000 pounds (3,200 kg). A person is no match for this huge and deadly hunter.

Great white sharks sometimes bite surfers. This is probably because the surfers look like seals from below. Seals are a favorite meal for great white sharks.

People are much more dangerous to sharks than sharks are to people. Fishermen kill about 100 million sharks each year. They do this because shark bodies provide many different products that people like. Sharkfin soup and sharkskin shoes are two popular products.

Some people also kill sharks just for fun. There are laws against this, but people do it anyway. The scalloped hammerhead shark

Caudal fins of blue sharks on drying racks

and other species are dying out because people kill too many of them.

Sharks face many other dangers. Ocean pollution and habitat destruction, for example, are hurting sharks around the world. Will these creatures survive another 450 million years? No one knows for sure. But one thing is certain. People fight to protect things they respect and understand. This means that every person who learns about sharks is helping to save these amazing animals.

Bull Shark

Glossary

Ancestors—Individuals from which descendants or later kinds evolved.

Bottom feeding—A method of hunting in which prey is caught on the ocean floor.

Carnivores—Animals that eat flesh.

Cartilage—A tough, rubbery tissue, which sharks' skeletons are made of.

Countershading—Body coloration in which an animal is darker on the top of its body and lighter on the bottom.

Filter feeding—A method of hunting in which plankton is pushed through a shark's gills and trapped in special plates.

Flexible—Able to be bent easily.

Lateral line—A body organ in fish that detects and interprets movements in water.

Migrate—Movement from one area of the world to another.

Plankton—Small and microscopic plants and animals that drift in large numbers in fresh- or salt water.

Pups—Newborn or young sharks.

Serrated—Having a notched edge, like a saw.

Snout—The projecting nose and jaws of an animal.

Streamlined—A body shape that allows easy movement through air or water.

Tropical—Climate with a warm temperature.

Vibrations—The shaking motions of an object that is moving.